Giuseppe Verdi
REQUIEM

in Full Score

Dover Publications, Inc.

New York

INSTRUMENTATION

The German terms and abbreviations used in the score appear here in square brackets.

WOODWINDS: 3 flutes [grosse Flöten; gr. Fl.] (player III also takes over the piccolo [kleine Flöte; kl. Fl.])—2 oboes [Oboen; Ob.]—2 clarinets [Klarinetten; Klar.]—4 bassoons [Fagotte; Fag.]

BRASS: 4 horns [Hörner; Hrn.]—4 trumpets [Trompeten; Trp.]—3 trombones [Posaunen; Pos.]—1 bass tuba [Basstuba; Tb.]

PERCUSSION: 3 kettledrums [Pauken; Pk.]—1 bass drum [grosse Trommel; Gr. Tr.]

STRINGS: Violins [Violinen; Viol.] I & II—Violas [Bratschen; Br.]—Violoncelli [Vc.]—double basses [Kontrabässe; Kb.]

In addition, there are 4 trumpets off.

PERFORMANCE TIME

No. 1.	Requiem	12 min.
No. 2.	Dies irae	40 min.
No. 3.	Offertorio	11 min.
No. 4.	Sanctus	4 min.
No. 5.	Agnus Dei	6 min.
No. 6.	Lux aeterna	9 min.
No. 7.	Libera me	15 min.

This Dover edition, first published in 1978, is an unabridged republication of the work as edited by Kurt Soldan and published by C. F. Peters, Leipzig, n.d. The German-language frontmatter has been translated into English for the present volume, and a glossary of German terms found in the score has been specially prepared.

International Standard Book Number: 0-486-23682-X
Library of Congress Catalog Card Number: 78-54773

Manufactured in the United States of America
Dover Publications, Inc.
31 East 2nd Street
Mineola, N.Y. 11501

REQUIEM

For four solo voices (soprano, mezzo soprano, tenor, bass), chorus and orchestra, by Giuseppe Verdi.

Composed 1874 for the first anniversary of the death of Alessandro Manzoni.

First performed in the church of San Marco, Milan, May 22, 1874 under the composer's direction.

CONTENTS

Glossary of German Terms

Here, in alphabetical order, are the indications (aside from instrumentation) placed in the present score by the German editor, along with English equivalents.

Alle: all; tutti

Alt (plural: *Alte*): alto(s)

As: A-flat

Äusserst leise, . . . traurig (p. 44): extremely softly, with somber voice and very sadly

B (note): B-flat

Bass (plural: *Bässe*): bass(es) (voices)

Breit und klagend: broadly, lamenting

Chor: chorus

Das Fell entspannt: slacken the head

Das Fell muss . . . gelingt (p. 19): the head must be well tightened so that these strokes on the weak beat are short but very loud

Das Fell stark entspannt: slacken the head quite a bit

Dasselbe Tempo . . . Achtelnote (p. 51): ♪ = preceding ♪

Des: D-flat

Die andere Hälfte: the other half

Die Hälfte: half

Die Sechszehntel langsam: take the sixteenth notes slowly

Dieser kleine Satz . . . Bässe (p. 196): this short phrase must continually be performed sotto voce and by only a few voices; in the chorus, 4 singers of each voice range are sufficient

düster: somberly

Ein Kontrabass allein: solo double bass

Entfernt und nicht getrennt: at a distance but in one group

Es: E-flat

gestopft: stopped

G. P. [*General-Pause*]: rest for all performers

H (note): B (natural)

h. d. Sz. [*hinter der Szene*]: off; not visible

Immer düster und . . .: continuing somber and . . .

je vier: four in each group

Klagend: lamenting

mit Dämpfer: muted

mit düsterer Stimme: with somber voice

ohne Dämpfer: remove mute

Sehr leise anfangend: beginning very softly

So leise wie möglich: as softly as possible

Sopran (plural: *Soprane*): soprano(s)

Tenor (plural: *Tenöre*): tenor(s)

u. [*und*]: and

Weinend: weeping

Wie eine Klage: like a lament

zu 2; zu 3: together; played by both (or, all three)

REQUIEM
(TOTENMESSE)
Nr. 1. Requiem

G. Verdi
(1813–1901)

3

4

Nr. 2. Dies iræ

*) NB. Entfernt und nicht getrennt

*) Das Fell muß gut gespannt sein, damit dieser Zwischenschlag kurz und sehr stark gelingt.

animando sempre sino alla fine, ma sempre poco a poco

*) Das Fell entspannt

Mors stu-pe-bit, mors stu-pe - bit et na-tu - ra, cum re-

sur - get cre - a-tu - ra, ju-di-can - ti re - spon-su - ra,

75

77

*) Das Fell muß gut gespannt sein, damit dieser Zwischenschlag kurz und sehr stark gelingt.

Nr. 3. Offertorio

Nr. 4. Sanctus

Nr. 5. Agnus Dei

Nr. 6. Lux æterna

155

Nr. 7. Libera me

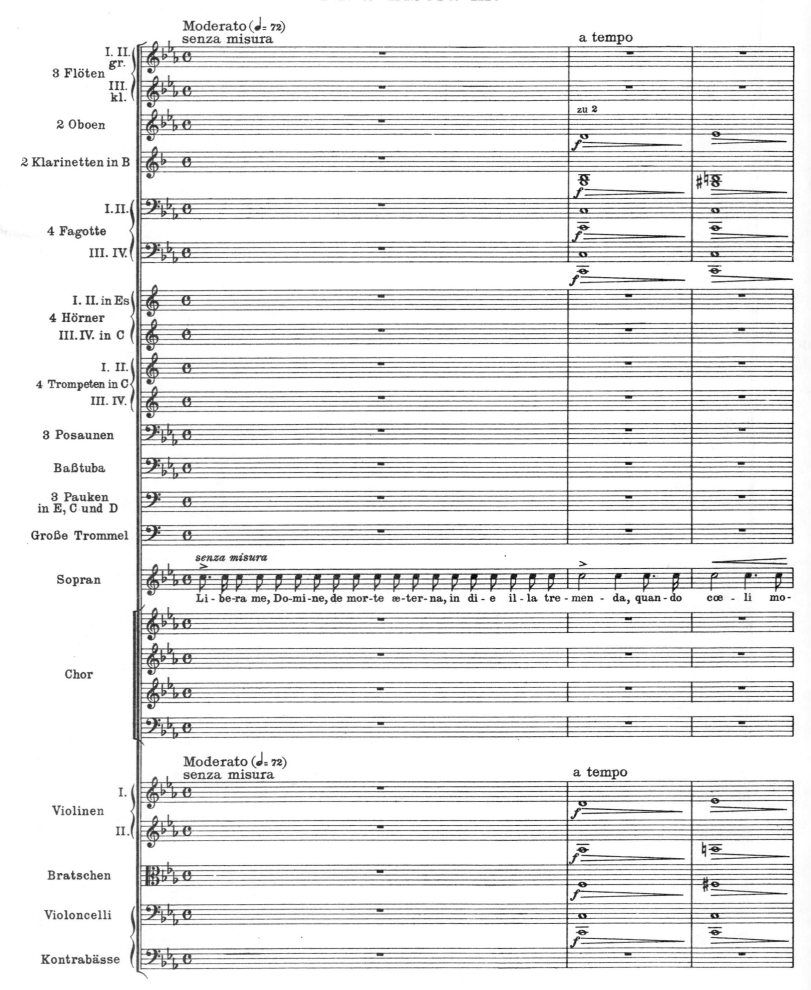

*) Das Fell muß gut gespannt sein, damit dieser Zwischenschlag kurz und sehr stark gelingt.

186

195

*) Dieser kleine Satz muß immer *sotto voce* und von wenigen Stimmen ausgeführt werden; im Chor genügen 4 Soprane, 4 Alte, 4 Tenöre und 4 Bässe.